THE ROLLING STONES
ROCK AND ROLL CIRCUS

THE SONGS

ENTRY OF THE GLADIATORS	10
SONG FOR JEFFREY	12
A QUICK ONE WHILE HE'S AWAY	18
OVER THE WAVES	30
AIN'T THAT A LOT OF LOVE	32
SOMETHING BETTER	40
YER BLUES	44
WHOLE LOTTA YOKO	58
JUMPING JACK FLASH	68
PARACHUTE WOMAN	74
NO EXPECTATIONS	82
YOU CAN'T ALWAYS GET WHAT YOU WANT	90
SYMPATHY FOR THE DEVIL	97
SALT OF THE EARTH	110

folio editor alisa ritz/art director iris keitel/cover illustration marvin mattelson/
design cody rasmussen/book design russell design associates/essay david dalton/concept lenne allik

7777 W. BLUEMOUND RD. P.O. BOX 13819 MILWAUKEE, WI 53213

In Association with abkco Music Inc.
Art & Design ©1995 ABKCO Records
Book ©1996 ABKCO Music, Inc.
ISBN 0-7935-7360-2
FOR ALL WORKS CONTAINED HEREIN: UNAUTHORIZED COPYING, ARRANGING, ADAPTING, RECORDING OR PUBLIC
PERFORMANCE IS AN INFRINGEMENT OF COPYRIGHT. INFRINGERS ARE LIABLE UNDER THE LAW.

1968... a very good year
By David Dalton, 1995

The Rolling Stones Rock and Roll Circus is a time capsule if ever there was one because here, as if found in a bottle washed up on the beach, are two classic days in December 1968 that in many ways capture the enthusiasms, aspirations and communal spirit of an entire era.

On December 10th and the early morning hours of the 11th, the Rolling Stones, John Lennon and Yoko Ono, Eric Clapton, Mitch Mitchell, the Who, Jethro Tull, Taj Mahal and Marianne Faithfull got together in a television studio in North London to record a TV special that has not been seen for twenty-eight years.

1968 was a very good year for rock 'n' roll. The rest of the world may have been going to pot, but rock was a runaway train, fulfilling every fantasy in the fevered teenage brain. The Beatles' "Sgt. Pepper's Lonely Hearts Club Band" had come out the previous year and raised the cultural stakes. Rock was no longer seen as mindless teenage noise; some critics were calling it a genuine art form. At UCLA, knowledge of the music of the Rolling Stones was now a requisite for obtaining a degree in musicology.

But the triumph of rock was not just an academic issue. In some circles it was seriously being touted as a sort of social panacea. After the Summer of Love and the Monterey Pop Festival — where hippies, radicals, Hell's Angels and cops mingled peacefully for three days — even quite sensible people were suggesting rock might be just the thing to unite a fractured world. Mick Jagger had actually been approached to run as a Labour Member of Parliament.

The Stones drug busts of the year before had mobilized the entire counterculture and many in the establishment as well. The acquittal of Mick and Keith was seen as an indictment of a corrupt establishment and made them into folk heroes. In May of '68 French students and workers charged police barricades with their new anthem, "Jumping Jack Flash," blasting on a thousand transistor radios.

We are, in other words, at mid-point of late sixties lunacy, shortly before the walls came tumbling down. A year on would come the apotheosis of sixties rock at Woodstock — followed shortly thereafter by Altamont, the quasi-official end of the sixties. But in December of 1968 millennial delusions were still rampant in sleepy old London town.

In 1968 London was the epicenter of the rock world. Here dwelt the crown princes of rock, the Beatles and the Rolling Stones. It was a sovereign teen domain where the adult world had been turned upside down. Rock stars were the new nobility. The dark princes of this realm were the Rolling Stones and they held court nightly in dingy clubs with clever names.

Neither the Beatles nor the Stones had been seen on stage for almost two years. While the Beatles were content to toil in multitrack studios, the Stones were anxious to get their ya-yas out on the street.

In November of 1968 the Stones were about to release their new album, Beggar's Banquet, a brooding blues-roots masterpiece filled with figures of mesmerizing fantasy, pulsing defiance and funk. It was the first in a series of classic Stones albums and, naturally, they wanted to proclaim it to the world.

The Stones had been pioneers in the making of outrageous rock videos. In 1966 there was the notorious "Have You Seen Your Mother, Baby" (featuring the band in drag) and in 1967 their sneering parody of the trial of Oscar Wilde, "We Love You." "Charlie Is My Darling" the film of their 1965 Irish tour runs a close second to "Don't Look Back" as a record of rock on the road. In 1968 alone the Stones released two stunning videos: "Jumping Jack Flash" and "Child of the Moon."

And so in November of 1968 Jagger began planning a filmed rock extravaganza with an eclectic mix of acts plus some element that would make the whole event more than just another rock concert — something festive for the holiday season!

Now it so happened that Mick loved circuses — especially the small, English travelling circuses with overweight acrobats and other dodgy acts dear to the hearts of English children. A circus would be romantic and nostalgic and just the right sort of haphazard surrealistic event to incorporate anything.

Initially Mick had wanted Brigitte Bardot to be the ringmaster but contractual obligations prevented her from appearing so Mick stood in for her.

You could have a fire-eater, or Ali Baba, and then just drop in — at key moments — your assorted British rock luminaries with amps and presto!

Mick got on the phone and within a week he rounded up the Who, Eric Clapton, Mitch Mitchell from the Jimi Hendrix Experience along with the relatively unknown Jethro Tull and from the USA, the blues singer, Taj Mahal. To enlist his girlfriend Marianne Faithfull he had only to shout to the next room.

Initially Mick had wanted Brigitte Bardot to be the ringmaster but contractual obligations prevented her from appearing so Mick stood in for her. For the other participants there were no such problems. Life was still simple enough and the sense of comraderie among the rock community in London real enough for the aristocracy of British rock to assemble at a moment's notice without drawn-out negotiations.

Allen Klein, the Stones manager put up the money for the show. Was there anything missing from the festivities? Well, a Beatle would be nice. Now, if only John Lennon could be persuaded to run away and join the circus.

"I called Lennon's home number," Klein recalls. "His answering machine had a message to the tune of 'Three Blind Mice' which went 'We're not home, we're not home. If you leave a message we'll call you back — maybe.'"

Michael Lindsay-Hogg, who had been a director for the BBC's music TV show, Ready, Steady, Go! (and was currently filming the Beatles' Let It Be at Twickenham Studios) was the obvious choice for a director and he, in turn, got the cinematographer Tony Richmond to sign on.

While Mick and Michael Lindsay-Hogg put their heads together to plan the show, feverish activity went on behind the scenes. Michael Lindsay-Hogg and Tony Richmond imported special cameras from France that would permit shooting film and video footage simultaneously (this would expedite the editing process). 400 brightly colored ponchos and hats were rented, a circus tent, ring, and other paraphernalia were ordered. Several tons of sawdust had to be delivered. Rehearsals for the musicians were held at the Londonderry Hotel on the two days before filming. The procedure was essentially this: whoever showed up would be included in the show.

The day of the show, December 10th, came. It began at ten in the morning. One by one and two by two trapeze artists, rock stars, crew and fans assembled at the cavernous Intertel TV studio in Wembley, North London. Not much

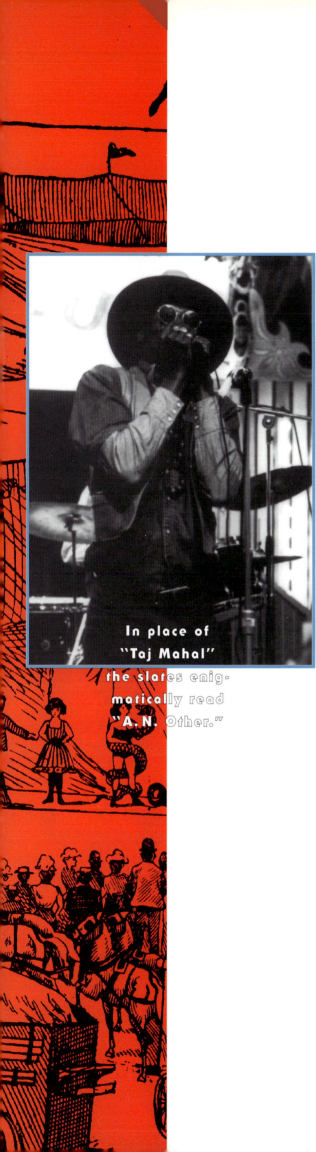

In place of "Taj Mahal" the slates enigmatically read "A. N. Other."

happened for the first few hours as the stages were set up. We sat around and watched the circus performers and clowns juggle and pratfall and wobble on the high wire.

This was never intended to be a professional circus with flawless acts that you might have seen on The Ed Sullivan Show. Part of the joy of these small circuses was how inept the performers were. Brits have always had a soft spot for the incompetent and third rate. They love to heckle them. This is the sort of circus you'd go to at the Moss Empire on August Bank Holiday with your granny, featuring bumbling jugglers and overweight acrobats and tumbling magicians. The type of performance where everyone would cheer when the monocyclist fell off his bike or the poodle refused to jump through the hoop.

Gradually the princes of rock began to arrive with their retinues in tow. Taj Mahal and his band were the first to be filmed. Mick had met him at the Whiskey A Go Go in LA the year before and was so keen on having him at the Circus he flew him in for the show. Because of conflicts with the British musicians union his presence in England had to be kept a secret. His name wasn't even used on the clapboards that recorded the different takes. In place of "Taj Mahal" the slates enigmatically read "A. N. Other."

Jagger found Jethro Tull through demo tapes sent to the Stones office by various bands.

In the context of all the gaudy, glittering costumes Marianne Faithfull looked like a crimson orchid in her floor length gown as Mick crouched beside her and held her hand as the crew set up to shoot her sequence. Her affectless delivery of "Something Better" seemed no more than an extension of her earlier Village of the Damned stage presence. "Something Better" was the B side of her new single (briefly released in February of 1969). The A side, "Sister Morphine," would have been a bit too macabre for so festive an occasion.

At 8 o'clock there was a two hour break for dinner after which it was time for the supergroup, The Dirty Mac, to go on. First a bit of banter between Mick and John Lennon. It was rivetting to watch the two prime movers of the scene having a go at each other. Lennon (the only person quicker on the uptake than Mick) behaving a tad condescendingly towards Jagger as he lobs a number of surreal non-sequiturs at him.

It was this sort of interchange of energy (and one-upmanship) that propelled the London rock scene. The concept of a rock concert as circus was clearly indebted

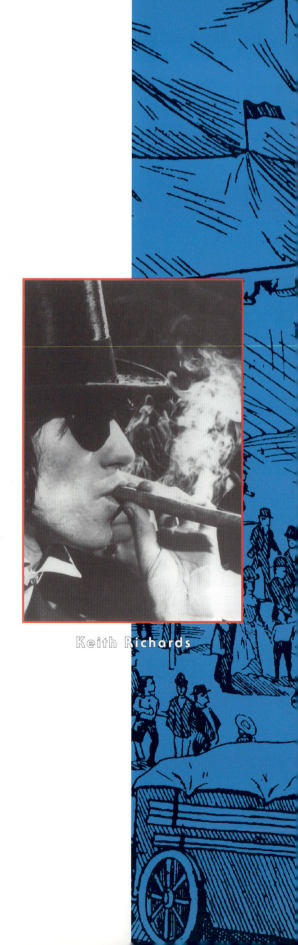

Keith Richards

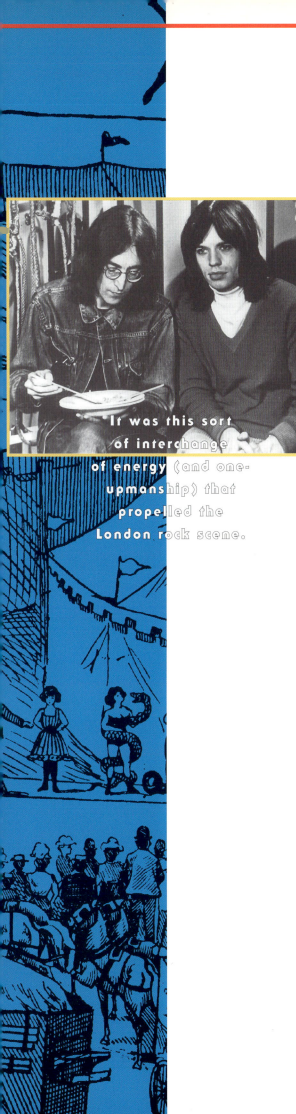

It was this sort of interchange of energy (and one-upmanship) that propelled the London rock scene.

to the Beatles "Being For the Benefit of Mr. Kite" on Sgt. Pepper, just as the marching band drollery and campy reprise at the end of "Something Happened To Me Yesterday" on the Stones album Between the Buttons had been one of the inspirations for Sgt. Pepper.

Most jams involving such stellar participants as the members of The Dirty Mac sound better in theory than in practice. But it is Lennon's ardor that burns away the perfunctory showboating endemic to most supergroups and the other musicians pick up on its infectious fericocity. This is, incidentally, one of the first public performances that Lennon did with Yoko Ono and it led to the live piece John and Yoko were to do in Canada the following year.

About 11:00pm The Who came on. Having just come off the road they were on top form. Pure, mad thrashing energy. Sweat pouring off Keith Moon like Shiva with a hundred arms. They performed their mini opera, "A Quick One While He's Away," so flawlessly it was easy to overlook how quirky it was. While still well within the context of rock 'n' roll, its linked segments, alternating lyricism and pounding rock are a sign of the preposterous hubris of the day: the attempt to transcend rock. (Hah!)

Around midnight Ian Stewart, the Stones road manager, sometime pianist (and founding member), began setting up the Stones' equipment. John Lennon's signing — which introduces the Stones — was actually shot on another day on the set of the Beatles' film, Let It Be, being filmed at the same time.

Even though the Stones were obviously tired by the time they went on — it was by now some fourteen hours into the event — the Circus lurched into yet another gear when the Stones began playing. There was the additional pleasure of seeing the Stones playing some of their old songs to warm up and then head right into that fable of their fantasy history, their single "Jumping Jack Flash," then on through two songs from Beggars Banquet: "Parachute Woman," and "No Expectations." Mick sang "You Can't Always Get What you Want" (from their upcoming album, "Let It Bleed") directly to Marianne Faithfull.

Around three thirty in the morning there was a long break. Exhaustion had set in and patience was running out all over the place. The equanimious English temperament was being sorely tried. Things were getting lost.

But all lethargy vanished when around five o'clock Rocky Dijon began tapping on the congas, Brian Jones rattled the marimbas, Charlie's drums kicked in and "Sympathy For the

Devil" began its ominous syncopated prowl. We were in a jungle clearing in Brazil at a macumba ceremony with Papa Legba Mick summoning up ferocious specters, the most chilling of all being the one he summons out of himself, prancing, lurching, flaunting himself in narcissistic fury, driven by the fevers of electricity to metamorphose before our eyes into an apparition of Lucifer awoken at a seance of the blues. The Stones Lucifer may be a bogey man out of a pantomime, but Keith's lethal guitar and Mick's wanton act of possession give the kiss of life to Beelzebub.

The revels ended on a rousing note. Everybody donned capes and hats and spirits rose to the occasion as the Stones sat down in the audience to sing "Salt of the Earth." Everyone joined in on the last chorus and Mick whimsically bade all adieu with: "There's nothing left for us to say but one good-nightly night."

And then, suddenly, it was all over. Doors opened to the outside and the sharp light of day like tiny gray daggers pitted our artificial paradise and broke the spell. Despite the last-helicopter-out-of-Saigon atmosphere of the final hours, no one, except possibly the crew, seemed relieved that it was over.

As time went by a large body of rumor has grown up as to what happened to The Rock and Roll Circus. The truth is that the Stones weren't happy with their performance. Various plans were made to reshoot the Stones segment, the most promising idea involved filming it at the coliseum in Rome, other locations were also considered, time moved on, Brian Jones died, and the moment had passed.

In retrospect, the Stones look pretty great. Their performance in the Circus is far less formal than what we usually see in their videos or on stage. But precisely because they are more relaxed we get to see the fluid relationship the Stones have to their music, slipping in and out of character, sending themselves up, goofing around. And then, just when you think it's all simply theater, Keith's ice pick guitar strikes a nerve, the rhythm section plugs in and the music reaches up, grabs Mick by the ankle and pulls him under.

The Rock and Roll Circus captures the delirious optimism of an era. Depending on your point of view it was either the high point in the history of the cosmos or a period of mass hallucination (or both). But call it what you will, for a brief moment it seemed that rock 'n' roll would inherit the earth.

— **David Dalton**

The Stones Lucifer may be a bogey man out of a pantomime, but Keith's lethal guitar and Mick's wanton act of possession give the kiss of life to Beelzebub.

Collage: Mick Rock

Entry of the Gladiators

Music by Julius Fucik

MICK JAGGER: "You've heard of Oxford Circus; you've heard of Piccadilly Circus; and this is The Rolling Stones Rock and Roll Circus: and we've got sights and sounds and marvels to delight your eyes and ears; and you'll be able to see the very first one of those in a few moments."

* Horns arr. for gtr.
** Chord symbols reflect overall tonality.

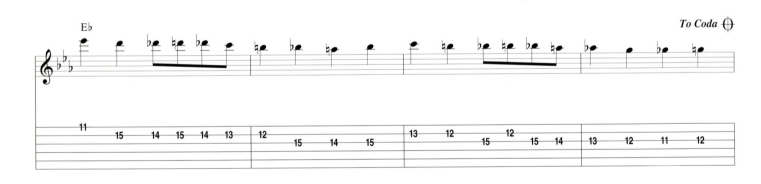

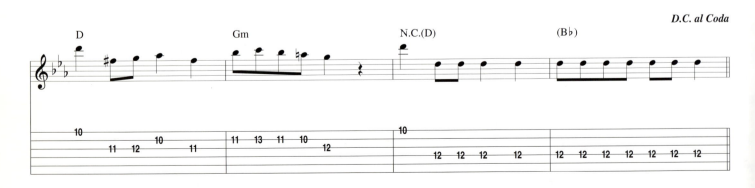

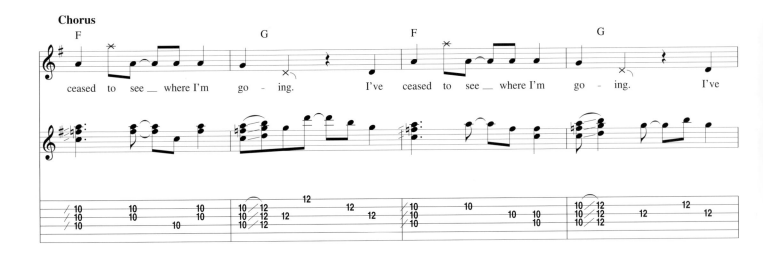

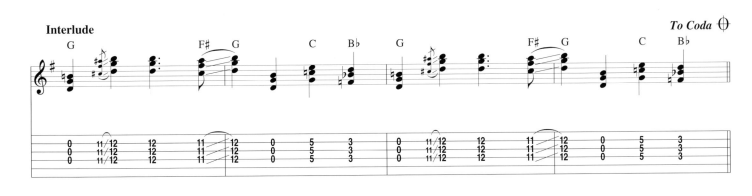
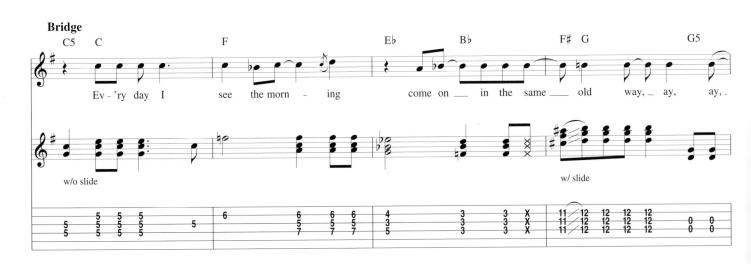

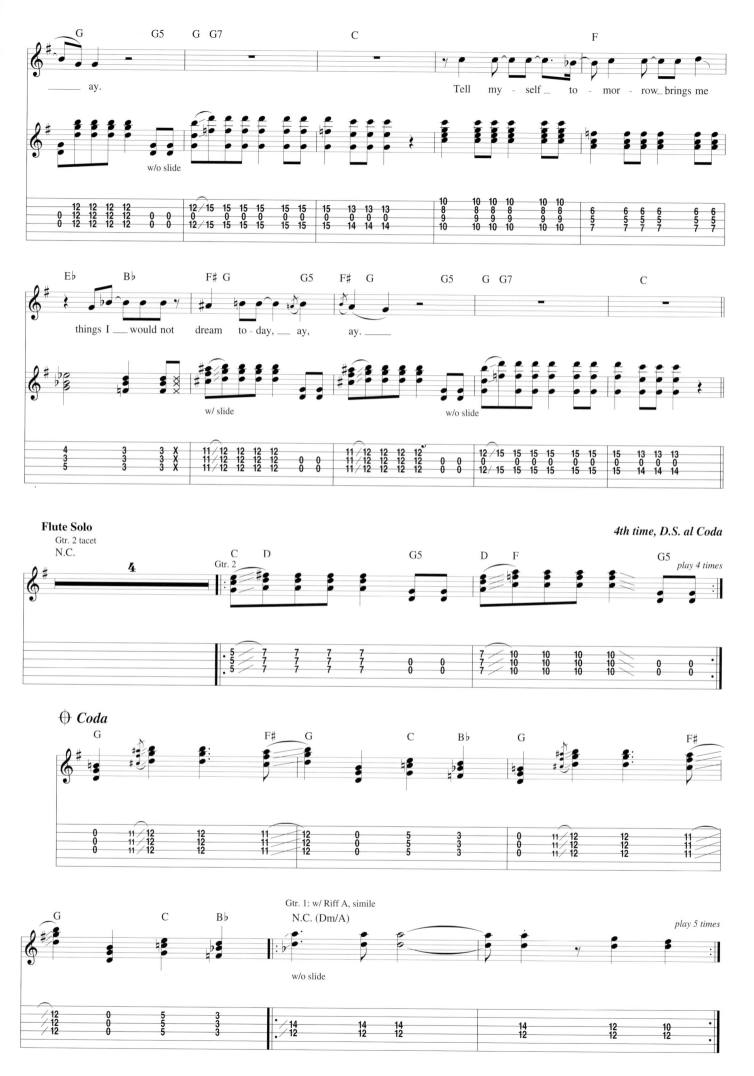

...g for Jeffrey

...ds and Music by Ian Anderson

...g to lose my way to tomorrow,
...g to get away in my car.
...ke you along with me
...ou would not go so far.
... see what I do not want to see,
...'t hear what I don't say.
...'t be what I don't want to be,
...tinue on my way.
...'ve ceased to see where I'm going.
...'ve ceased to see where I'm going.
...'ve ceased to see where I'm going.
...ll I don't want to.
... day I see the morning
... on in the same old way.
...myself tomorrow brings me
... I would not dream today.

Jethro Tull

The Who

A Quick One While He's Away

Words and Music by Peter Townshend

HER MAN'S BEEN GONE
Her man's been gone for neigh on a year.
He was due home yesterday, but he ain't here.
CRYING TOWN
Down your street your cryin' is a well-known sound.
Your street is very well known
Throughout your town.
Your town is famous for the little girl
Whose crying can be heard all around the world.
WE HAVE A REMEDY
We have a remedy you'll appreciate.
No need to be so sad, he's only late.
He'll bring you flowers and things,
Help pass your time.
We'll give him eagle's wings, then he can fly to you.
We have a remedy. Fa, la, la, la, la, la, la.
We have a remedy.
Little girl guide, why don't you stop your crying?
Here comes Ivor the dirty old sooty engine driver
To make you feel alright.
IVOR THE ENGINE DRIVER
My name is Ivor. I'm an engine driver.
I know him well. I know why you feel blue.
Just 'cause he's late
Don't mean he'll never get through.
He told me he loves you.
He ain't no liar, I ain't either.
So let's have a smile for an old engine driver.
SOON BE HOME
Soon be home, we'll soon be home.
We'll soon, we'll soon, soon, soon be home.
Soon be home, soon be home.
YOU ARE FORGIVEN
Dang! Dang! Dang! Dang!
Cello, cello, cello, cello, cello, cello, cel.
I can't believe it. Do my eyes deceive me?
Am I back in your arms? Away from all harm.
It's like a dream to be with you again.
Can't believe that I'm with you again.
I missed you and I must admit
I kissed a few and once did sit
On Ivor the engine driver's lap,
And later with him had a nap.
You are forgiven. You are forgiven.
You know you're forgiven, yeah. You are forgiven.

Ain't That a Lot of Love

Words and Music by Willia Dean Parker and Homer Banks

You got to dig it, baby. Yes, yes, yes,
You know the desert could not hold
All the love that I have in my heart for you.
If I could spread it out across the sea,
I know my love would cover it all up baby.
    Ain't that a lot of love
      For two hearts to have and hold?
If the bees only knew how sweet your love was,
They'd pack up their honeycomb.
If the birds overheard how sweet your voice was
Darlin', they would pack up their song, yeah.
(To Chorus)
Woman, now you, you gotta smile.
Now you gotta kiss.
You got a kindness, baby.
And you gotta lovin', lovin', lovin', baby.
(To Chorus)
Now if the cooks in the kitchen
Had a dress as tight as yours,
They would not need a fire.
Ain't a word I could say just to just to describe
Your fine looks of love, love and desire.
(To Chorus)
Woman, mama, ain't that a kindness?
Baby, baby ain't that a kindness?
Woman, woman ain't that a kindness?
Somebody, somebody tell me.
Somebody, somebody please.
Somebody, somebody somewhere.
Somebody, somebody tell this poor boy, children.
Somebody, somebody somewhere.
We got to bring it all together, people.
We got to do it all together, baby.

Taj Mahal

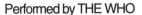
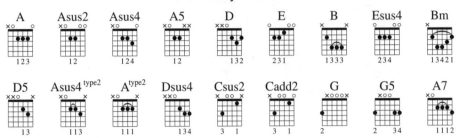

KEITH RICHARDS: "And now ladies and gentlemen, dig the Who."

HER MAN'S BEEN GONE

Her man's been gone for nigh on the year. He was due home yes-

-ter-day, but he ain't here. Her man's been gone for nigh on the

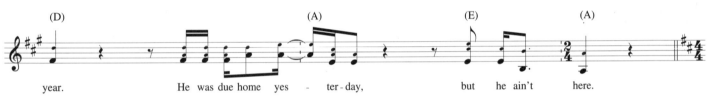

year. He was due home yes-ter-day, but he ain't here.

CRYING TOWN

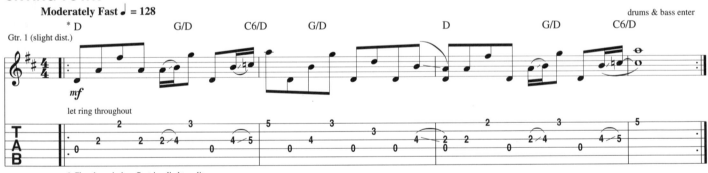

*Chord symbols reflect implied tonality.

Down your street your cry-in' is a well-known sound.

WE HAVE A REMEDY

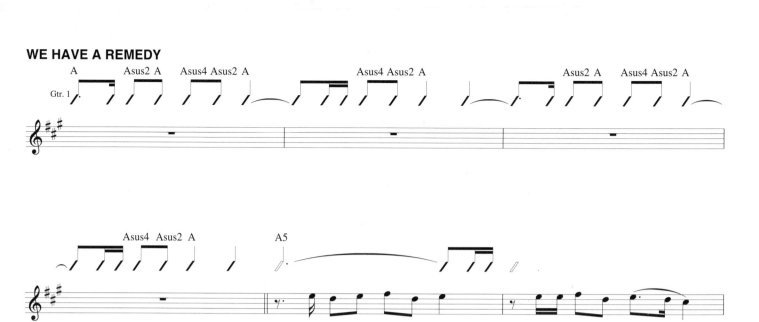
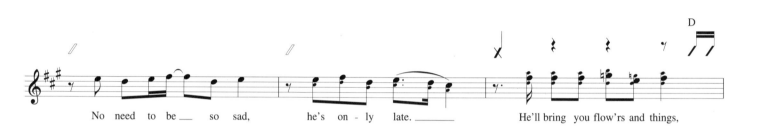

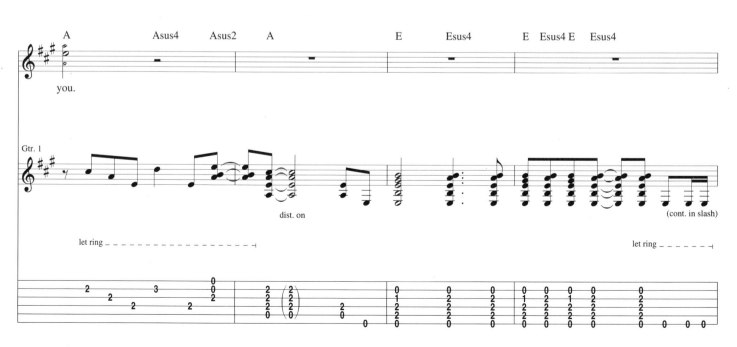

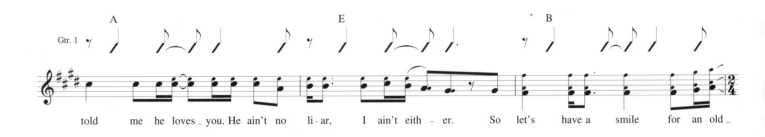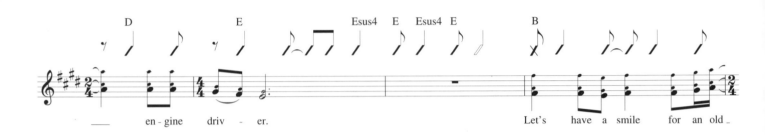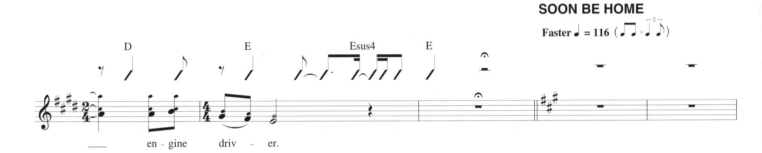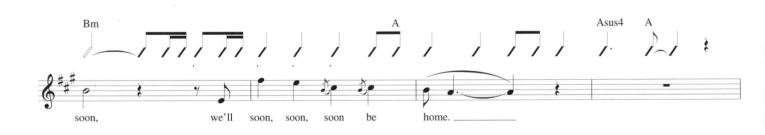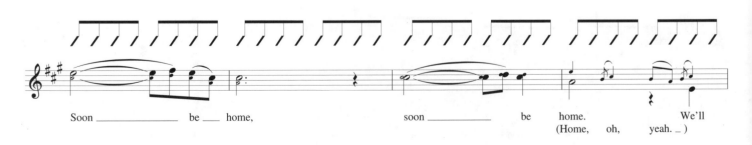

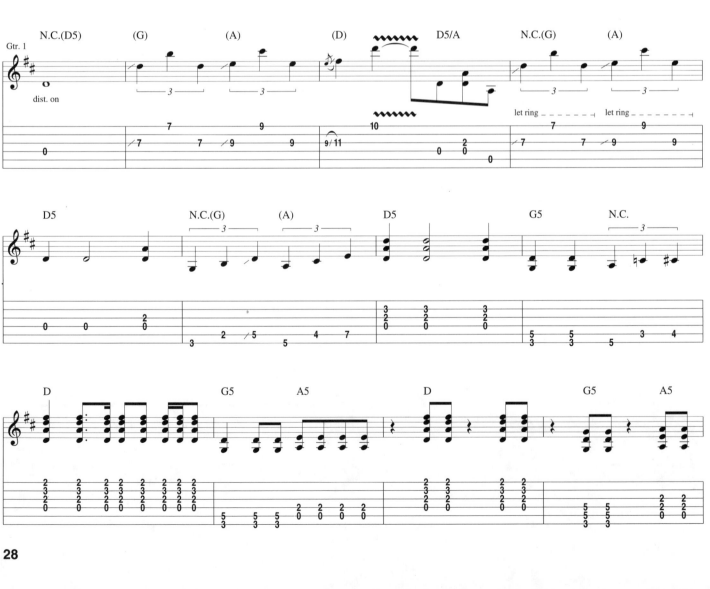

Over the Waves

Music by Juventino Rosas

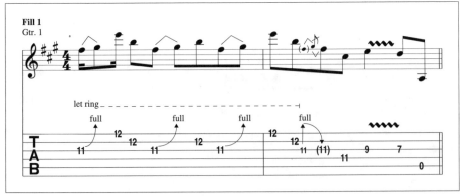

Something Better

Words and Music by Gerry Goffin and Barry Mann

Performed by MARIANNE FAITHFULL

CHARLIE WATTS: "And now we'd like to welcome our next guest, the beautiful Miss Marianne Faithfull."

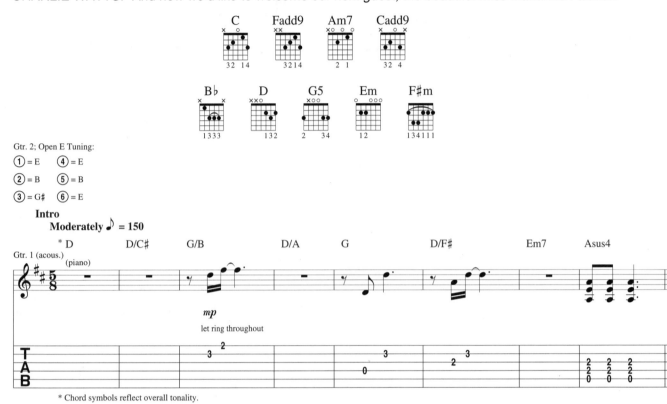

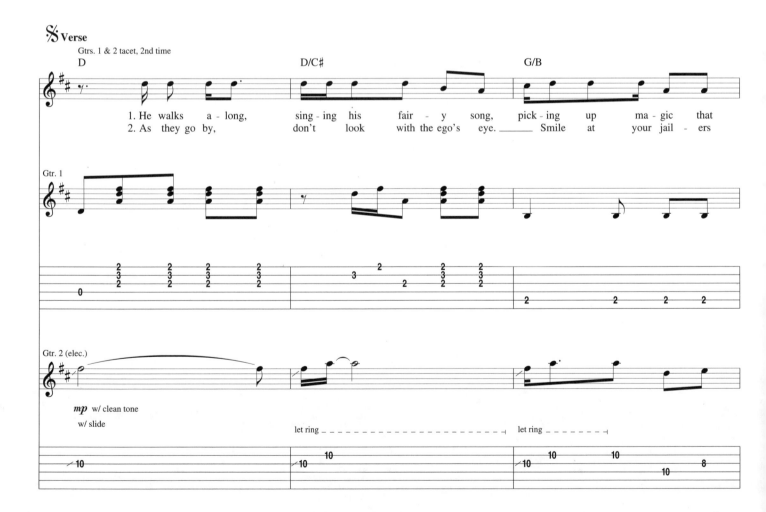

© 1969, 1971 SCREEN GEMS-EMI MUSIC INC.
All Rights Reserved International Copyright Secured Used by Permission

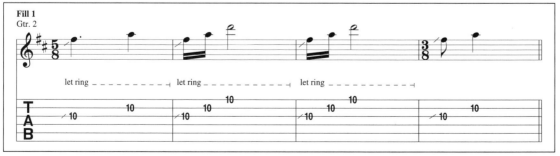

Yer Blues

Words and Music by John Lennon and Paul McCartney

Performed by THE DIRTY MAC

MICK JAGGER: "Winston, welcome to the show."

JOHN LENNON: "Michael, it's a pleasure to be here."

MICK JAGGER: "It's really nice to have you John. As you know I've admired your work for so long and... haven't been able to get together with you as much as I want..."

JOHN LENNON: "It's not been my fault, Michael."

MICK JAGGER: "Ah, do you remember that old place off Broadway we..."

JOHN LENNON: "Oh, those were the days, I want to hold your man. Remember that."

MICK JAGGER: "John, I want to talk to you about your new group, the, ah, Dirty Mac, that you got together for tonight's show, comprised of yourself..."

JOHN LENNON: "Sure...Well...myself, that's Winston Legthigh, you know and we've got Mitch Mitchell from The Jimi Hendrix Experience."

MICK JAGGER: "Are you really...experienced?"

JOHN LENNON: "Yeah really, oh very, very. You've read my file. And we've got Eric Clapton from The Cream, the late great Cream, Michael."

MICK JAGGER: "Cream...Fantastic."

JOHN LENNON: "And we've got Keith Richard, your own soul brother."

MICK JAGGER: "Dirty."

JOHN LENNON: "Great. I'd like just to give you this, Mike, on behalf of the British public."

MICK JAGGER: "Thank you, John. 'Yer Blues,' John. 'Yer Blues,' John."

JOHN LENNON: "Same to you, Michael."

MICK JAGGER: "'Yer Blues,' John."

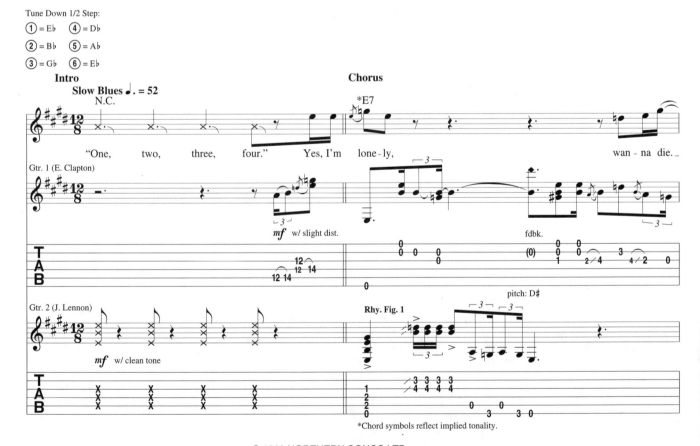

© 1968 NORTHERN SONGS LTD.
All Rights Controlled and Administered by EMI BLACKWOOD MUSIC INC. under license from SONY/ATV SONGS LLC
All Rights Reserved   International Copyright Secured   Used by Permission

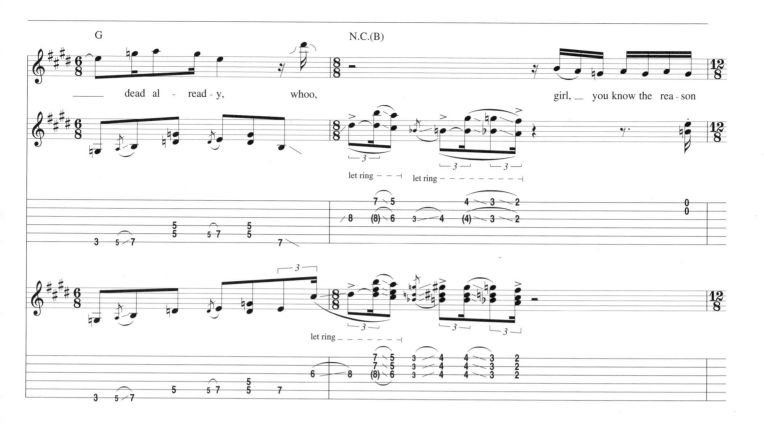
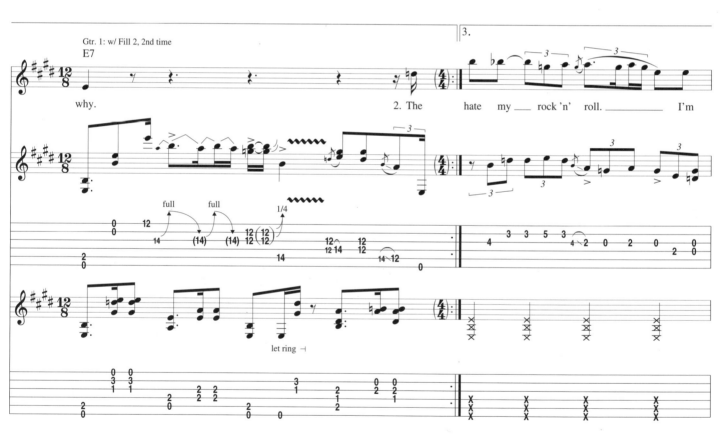
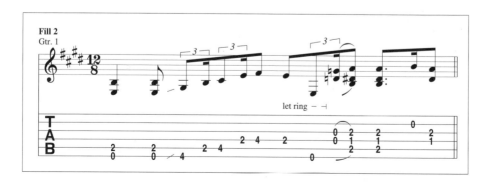

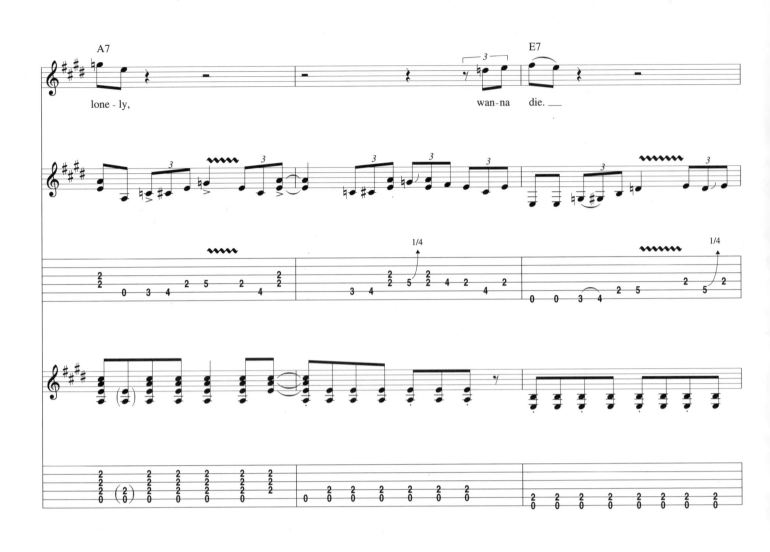
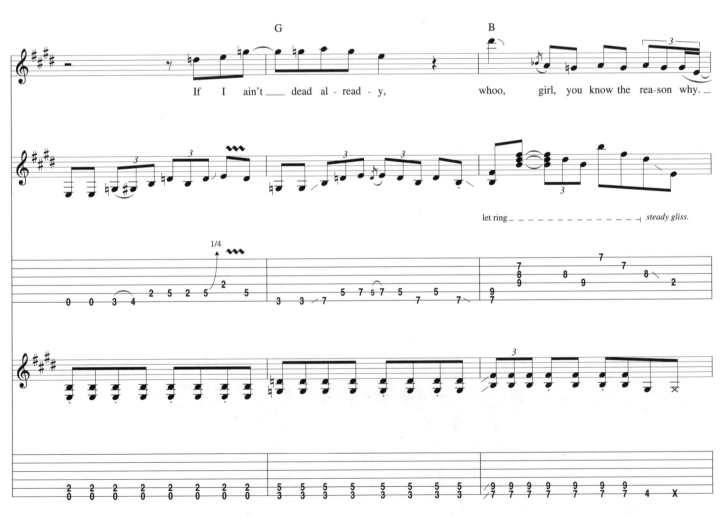

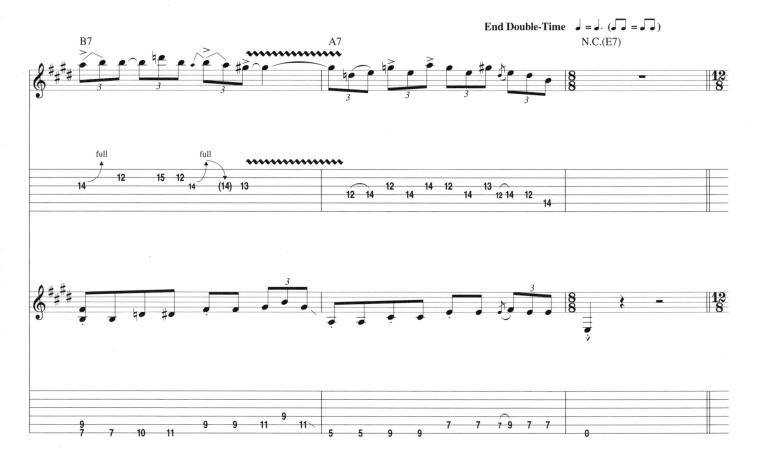

Outro

...wan - na die. Yes, I'm

*Vocals are barely audible at this point.

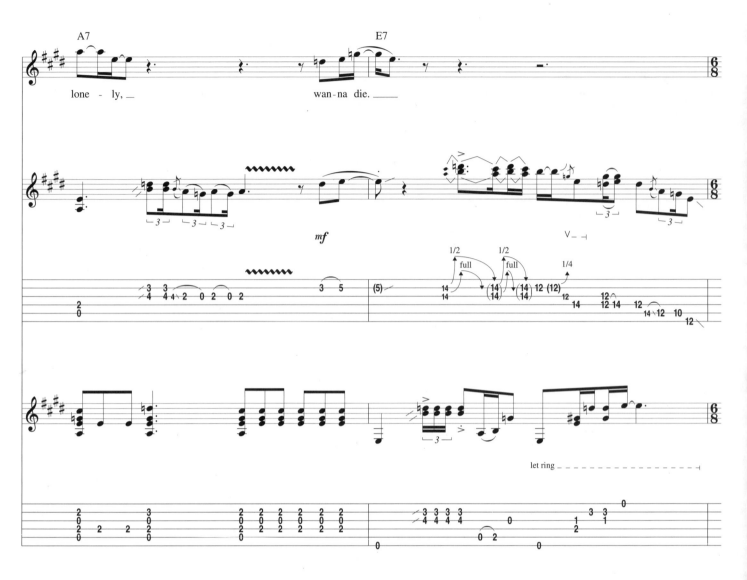
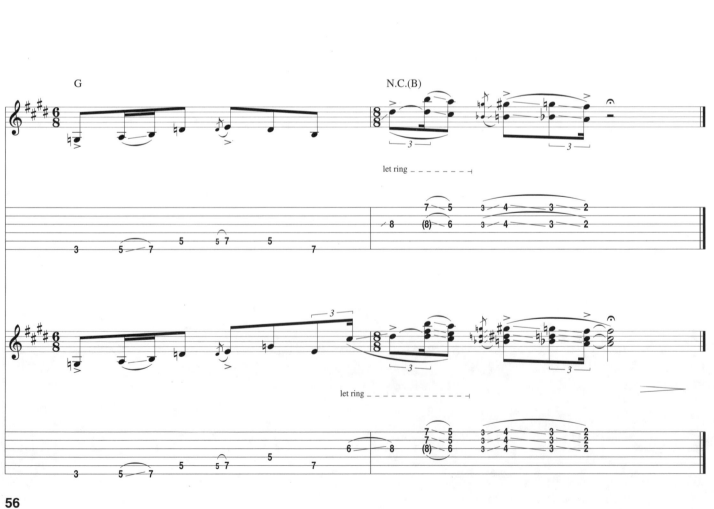

Something Better

Words and Music by
Gerry Goffin and Barry Mann

...lks along, singing his fairy song
...up magic that grows at his feet.
...ys her say in her peculiar way,
...ing good fortune on everyone's street.
..., hey, have you heard? Blue whiskey's the rage.
...send you a jug in the mornin'.
...s absured to live in a cage.
...know there's got to be somethin' better.
...y go by, don't look with the ego's eye.
...at your jailers until they grow weak.
...g can compare
...nething that's almost there,
...erry plum madness that all of us seek.

arianne Faithfull

The Dirty Mac

Yer Blues
Words and Music by
John Lennon and Paul McCartney

Yes, I'm lonely, wanna die.
Yes, I'm lonely, wanna die.
If I ain't dead already,
Girl, you know the reason why.
In the mornin', wanna die.
In the evenin', wanna die, yeah.
If I ain't dead already,
Girl, you know the reason why.
My mother was of the sky,
My father of the earth,
But I am of the universe
And you know what it's worth.
(To Chorus)
The eagle picks my eye,
The worm, he licks my bones,
Feel so suicidal,
Just like Dylan's Mister Jones.
(To Chorus)
Black cloud crossed my mind,
Blue mist 'round my soul,
Feel so suicidal,
Even hate my rock 'n' roll.
(To Chorus)

Whole Lotta Yoko
By Yoko Ono

Ah. Ah, ah. Ah,hi, ee. Ah, ah. Ah. *etc.*
Give me, give me, give me.

Yoko Ono &
Ivry Gitlis

Jumping Jack Flash
Words and Music by
Mick Jagger and Keith Richards

I was born in a crossfire hurricane.
And I howled at my ma in the driving rain.
But it's all right now. In fact it's a gas!
But it's all right. I'm Jumping Jack Flash.
It's a gas! Gas! Gas!
I was raised by a toothless, bearded hag.
I was schooled with a strap right across my back.
(To Chorus)
I was drowned. I was washed up and left for dead.
I fell down to my feet and I saw they bled.
I frowned at the crumbs of a crust of bread.
I was crowned
With a spike right through my head.
(To Chorus)

Parachute Woman
Words and Music by
Mick Jagger and Keith Richards

Parachute woman, land on me tonight.
Parachute woman, land on me tonight.
Yeah, I'll break big in New Orleans
And I'll spill over in Caroline.
Parachute woman, join me for a ride.
Parachute woman, join me for a ride.
Well, I'll make my play in Dallas
And get hot again in half the time.
Parachute woman, will you blow me out?
Parachute woman, will you blow me out?
Well, my heavy throbber's ichin'
Just to lay a solid rhythm down.

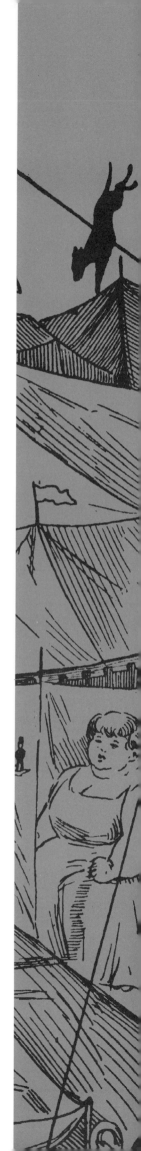

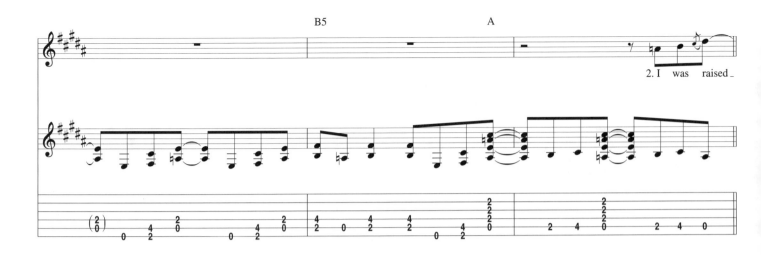

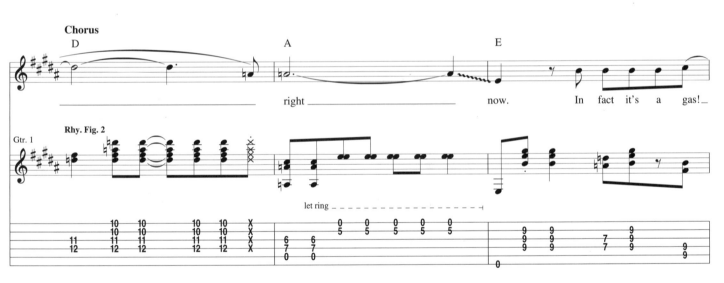
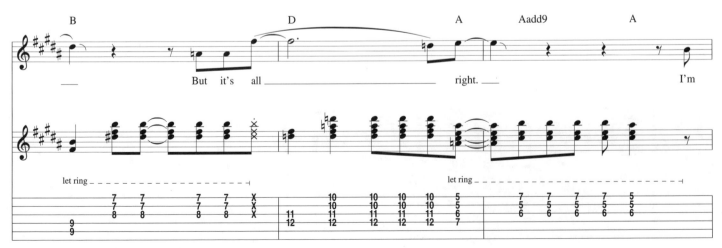

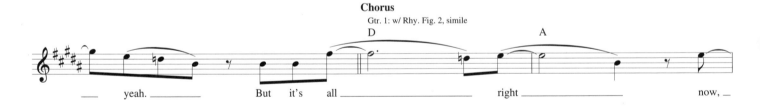
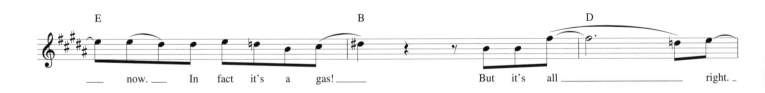

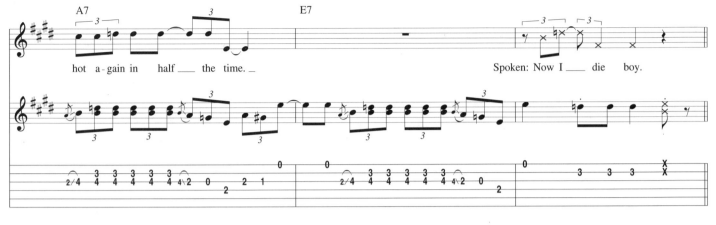
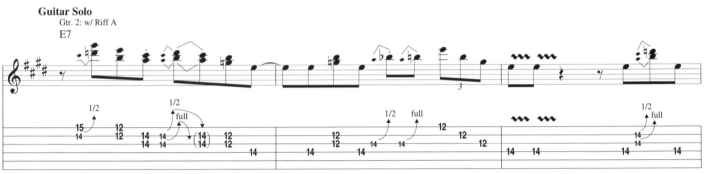
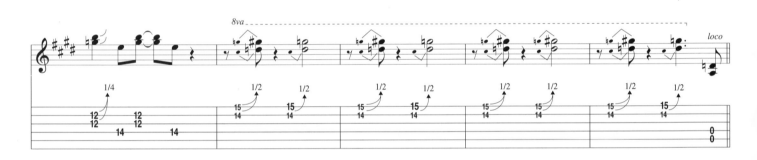

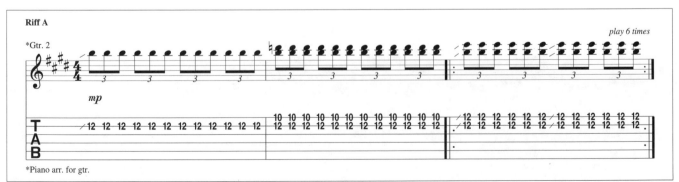

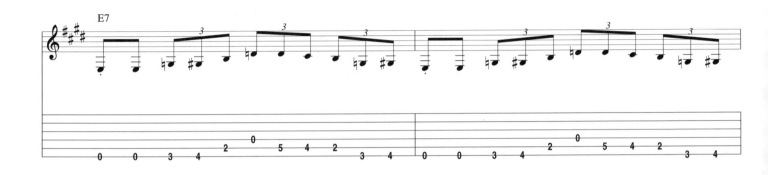
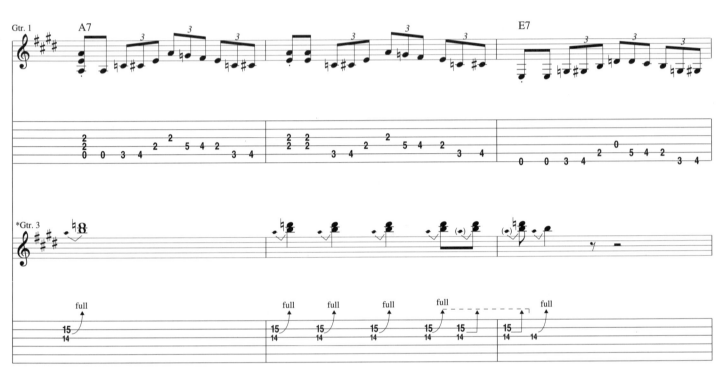

*Harmonica arr. for gtr.

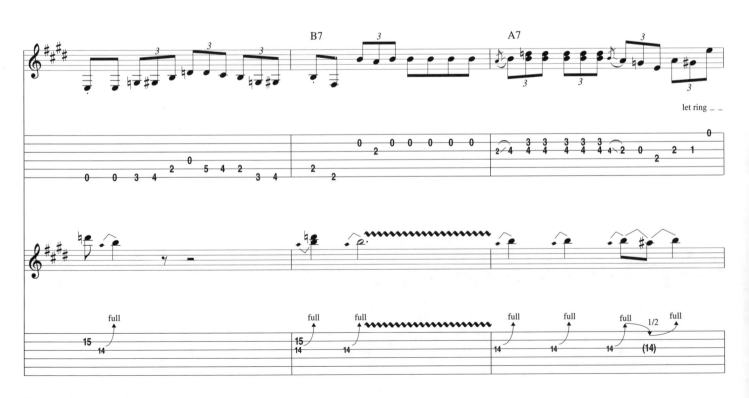

Outro-Guitar Solo

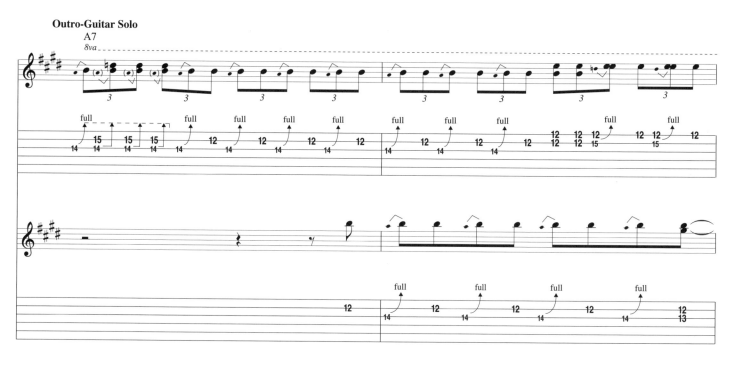

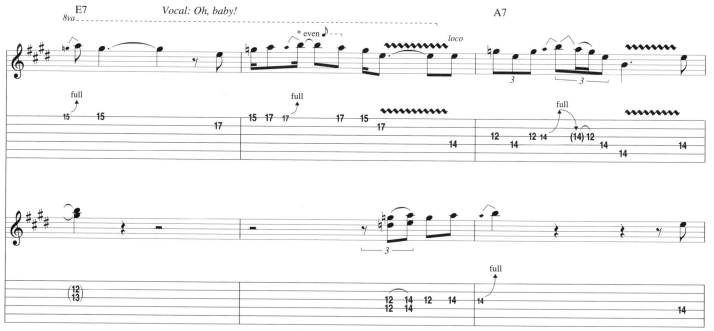

*Played as even eighth notes.

Expectations

Words and Music by
Mick Jagger and Keith Richards

Take me to the station
And put me on the train.
I've got no expectations
To pass through here again.
Once I was a rich man,
Now I am so poor.
But never in my sweet short life
Have I felt like this before.
Your heart is like the diamond,
You throw your pearls at swine.
And as I watch you leavin' me,
You pack my peace of mind.
Our love was like the water
That splashes on a stone.
Our love is like our music,
It's here and then it's gone.
Take me to the airport
And put me on the plane.
I've got no expectations
To pass through here again.

You Can't Always Get What You Want

Words and Music by
Mick Jagger and Keith Richards

I saw her today at the reception,
A glass of wine in her hand.
I knew she was gonna meet her connection.
At her feet was a footloose man.
And I said that you can't always get
What you want, honey.
You can't always get what you want.
You can't always get what you want.
But if you try sometimes, well,
You might just find
You get what you need.
Went to the Chelsea Drugstore
To get your prescription filled.
I was standing in line with your friend Jimmy,
And man, did he looked pretty ill.
We decided that we would have a soda.
My fav'rite flavor is cherry red.
I sing my song to my friend Mister Jimmy.
And he said one word to me and that was
"Dead." (To Chorus)
I saw her today at the reception.
Her glass was a bleeding man.
She was practiced at the art of deception.
I could tell by her blood-stained hands.
(To Chorus)
No, you can't always get what you want.
No, you can't always satisfy your greed.
No, you can't always get what you want.
But if you try sometime you just might find,
You just might find you get what you need,
Oh, yeah, yeah.

Sympathy for the Devil

Words and Music by
Mick Jagger and Keith Richards

Please allow me to introduce myself,
I'm a man of wealth and taste.
I've been around for a long, long year,
Stolen many a man's soul and faith.
I was around when Jesus Christ
Had his moment of doubt and pain.
Made damn sure that Pilate
Washed his hands and sealed his fate.
   Pleased to meet you,
   Hope you guess my name.
   But what's puzzling you
   Is just the nature of my game.
Stuck around Saint Petersburg
When I saw it was time for a change.
Killed the Tzar and his ministers;
Anastasia screamed in vain.
I rode a tank, held a gen'ral's rank
When the blitzkrieg raged
And the bodies stank.
Pleased to meet you,
Hope you guess my name.
But what's 'fussing you
Is just the nature of my game.
I watched with glee while your kings and queens
Fought for ten decades for the Gods they made.
I shouted out, "Who killed the Kennedy's,"
When after all it was you and me.
So let me please introduce myself,
I'm a man of wealth and taste.
I lay traps for troubadors
Who get killed before they reach Bombay.
(To Chorus)
Just as ev'ry cop is a criminal
And all the sinners, Saints.
As heads is tails, just call me Lucifer,
Because I'm in need of some restraint.
If you meet me, have some courtesy,
Have some sympathy and some taste.
Use all your well learned politesse
Or I'll lay your soul to waste. (To Chorus)

Salt of the Earth

Words and Music by
Mick Jagger and Keith Richards

Let's drink to the hard-working people.
Let's think of the lowly of birth.
Raise your glass to the good and the evil.
Let's drink to the salt of the earth.
Say a prayer for the common foot soldier.
Spare a thought for his back-breaking work.
Spare a thought for his wife and his children
Who burn the fires and who still till the earth.
When I look into this faceless crowd,
A swirling mass of grey, blue, black and white,
They don't look real to me.
In fact, we all look so strange.
Raise your glass to the hard-working people.
Let's drink to the uncounted heads.
Let's think of the wavering millions
Who need leading but they're gamblers instead.
Spare a thought for the stay at home gozer
Whose empty eyes means his strain really shows.
At the rates of grey-suited grafters,
A choice of cancer or polio.
And when I look into this faceless crowd,
A swirling mass of grey and black and white,
Do we all look real to you,
Or do we look too strange?
Let's drink to the hard-working people.
Let's drink to the lowly of birth.
Spare a thought for the rag-tagged people.
Let's drink to the salt of the earth.
Let's drink to the hard-working people.
Let's drink to the salt of the earth.
Let's think of the two thousand million.
Let's think of the humble of birth.

The Rolling Stones

No Expectations

Words and Music by Mick Jagger and Keith Richards

Performed by THE ROLLING STONES

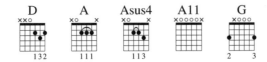

Gtr. 1; Open A Tuning:
① = E ④ = E
② = C# ⑤ = A
③ = A ⑥ = E

Intro
Moderately Slow ♩ = 78

Spoken: One, two, three, four.

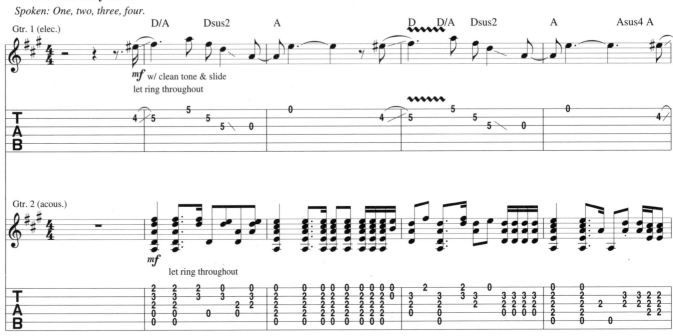

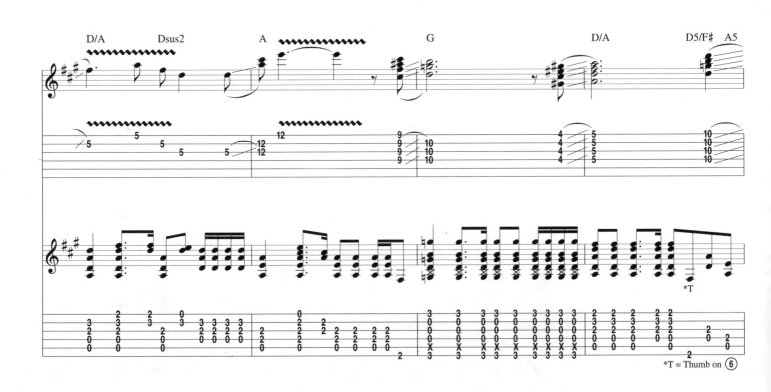

*T = Thumb on ⑥

© 1968 ABKCO Music, Inc. (Copyright Renewed)
1700 Broadway, New York, NY 10019
International Copyright Secured   All Rights Reserved

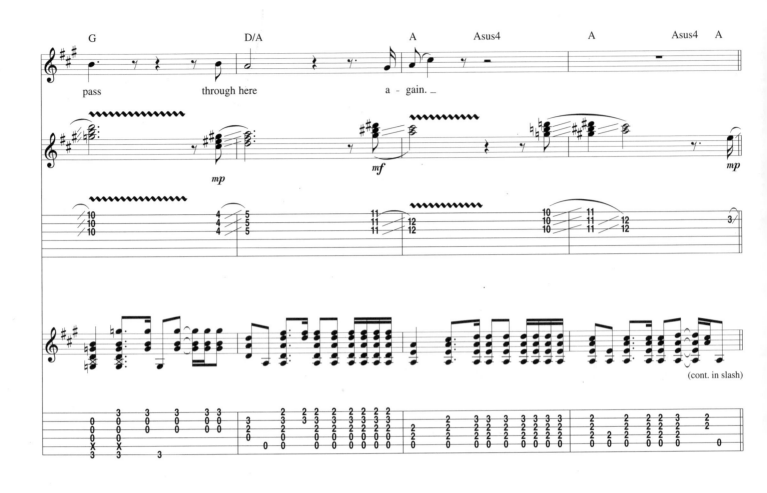

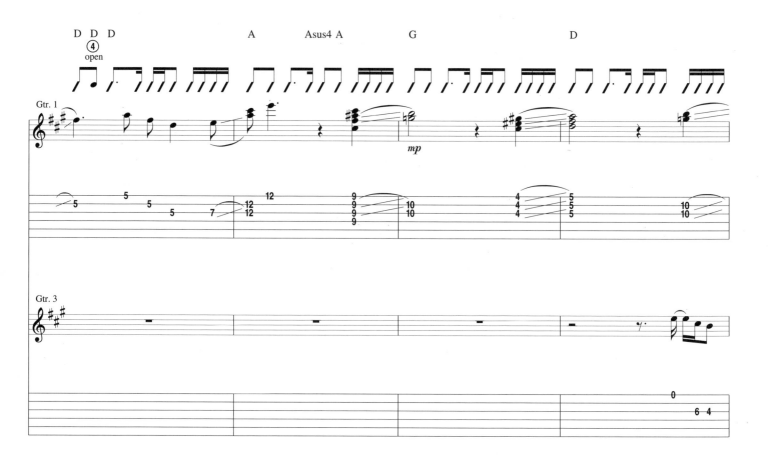
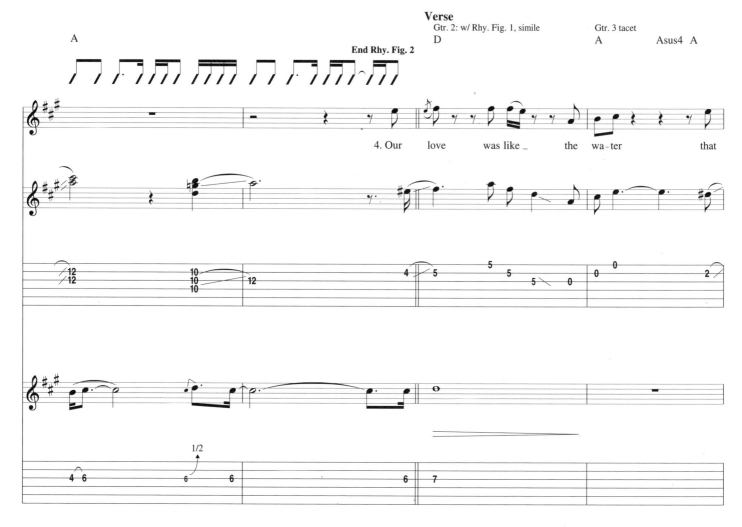

Outro

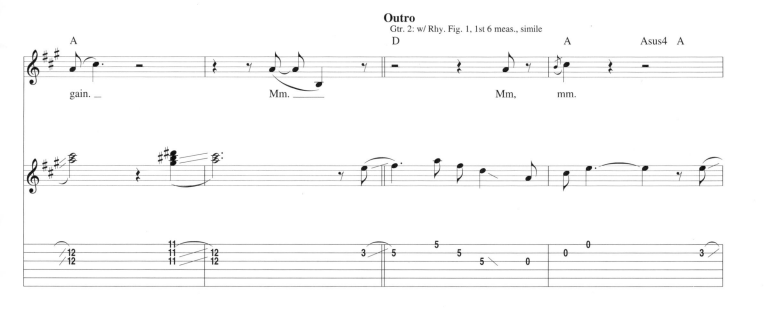

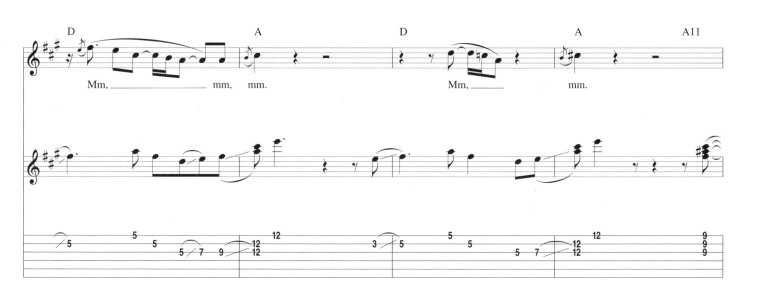

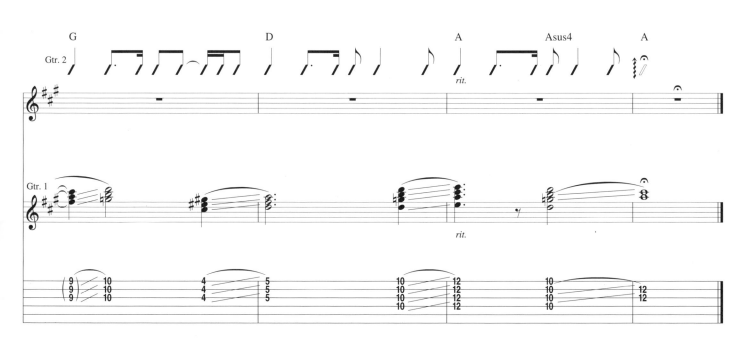

You Can't Always Get What You Want

Words and Music by Mick Jagger and Keith Richards
Performed by THE ROLLING STONES

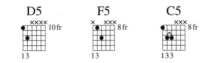

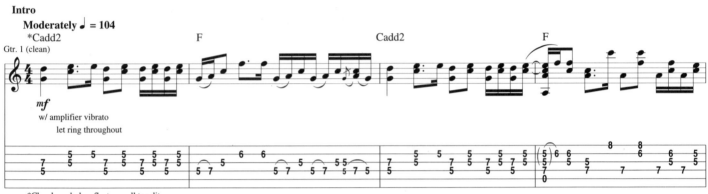

*Chord symbols reflect overall tonality.

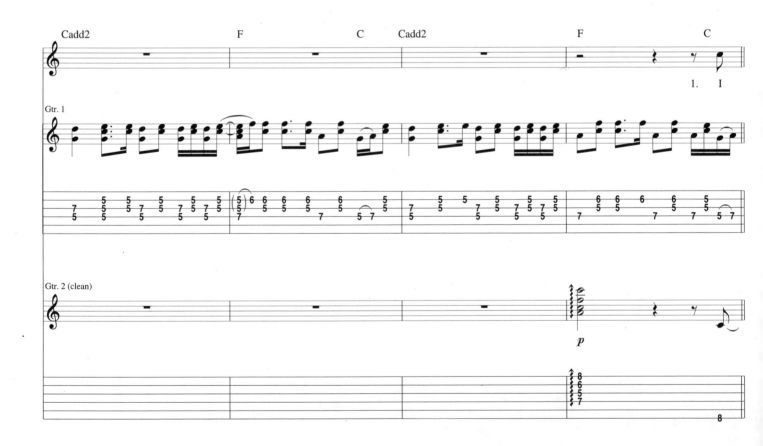

© 1969 ABKCO Music, Inc.
1700 Broadway, New York, NY 10019
International Copyright Secured   All Rights Reserved

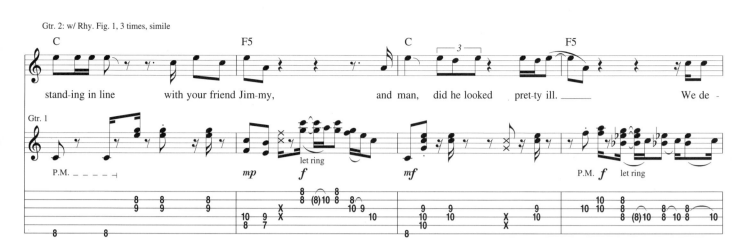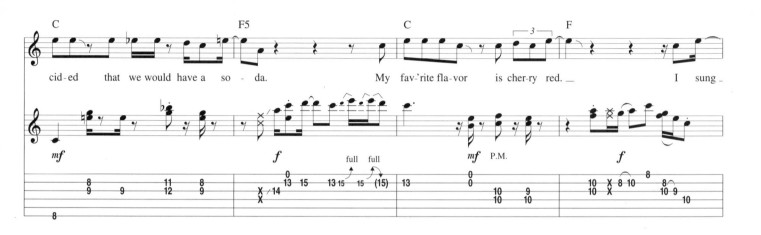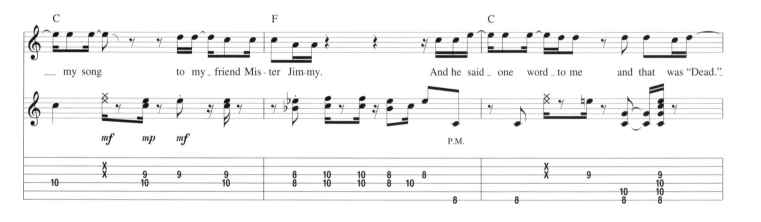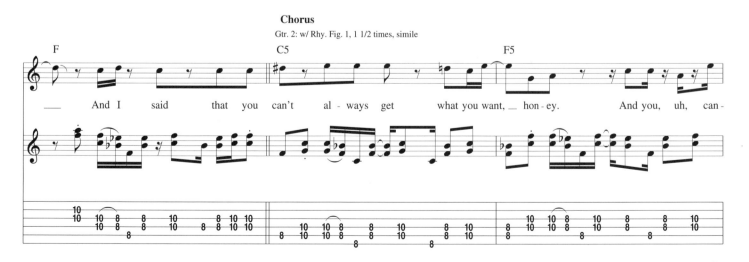

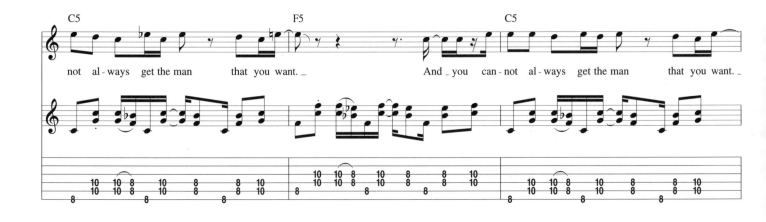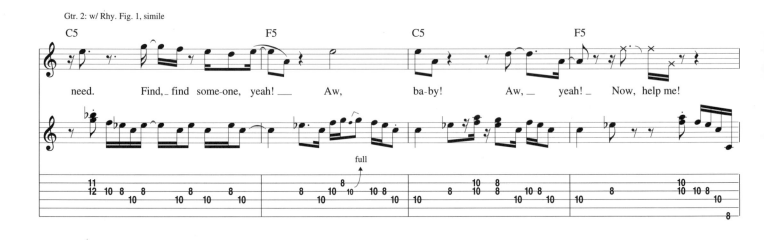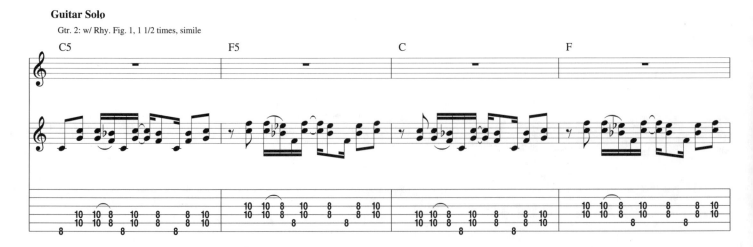

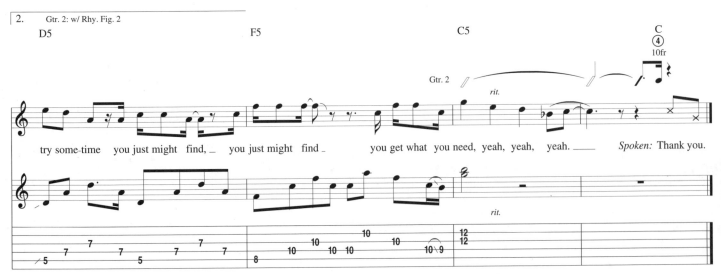

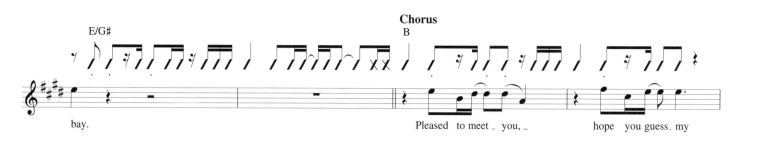
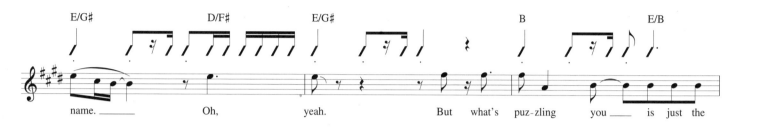
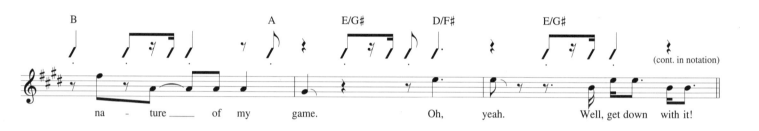
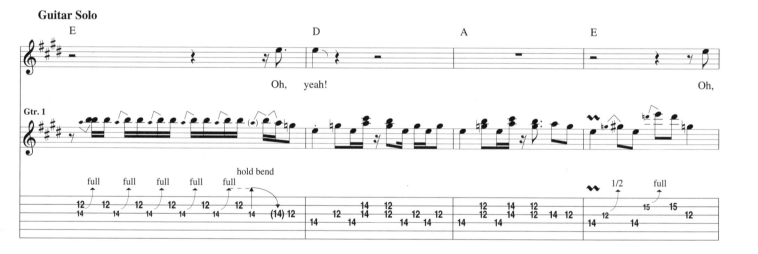
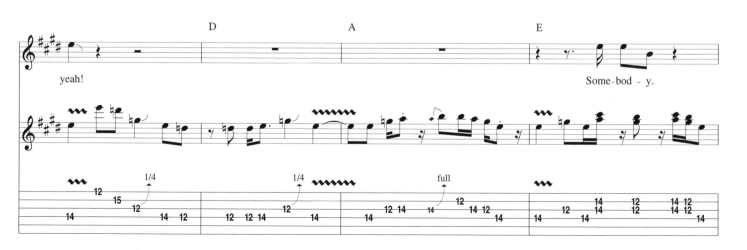

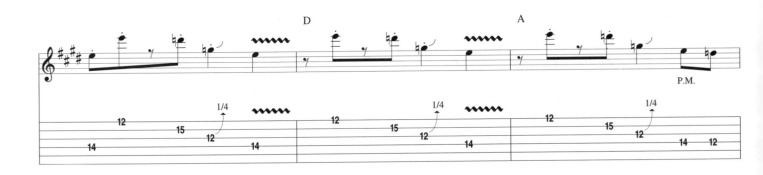

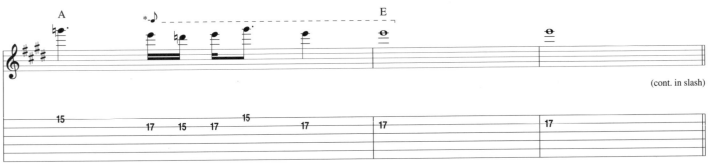

*Played behind the beat.

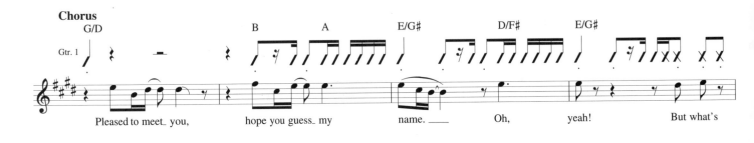
Pleased to meet_ you, hope you guess_ my name.___ Oh, yeah! But what's

puz-zling you___ is just the na-ture___ of my game. Yeah. 4. Just as

ev-'ry cop is a crim-i-nal,___ and all___ the sin-ners, Saints.___ As

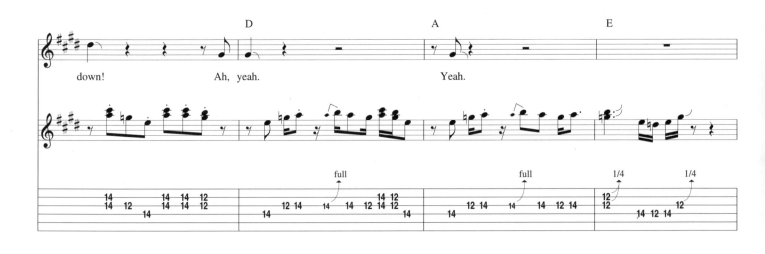
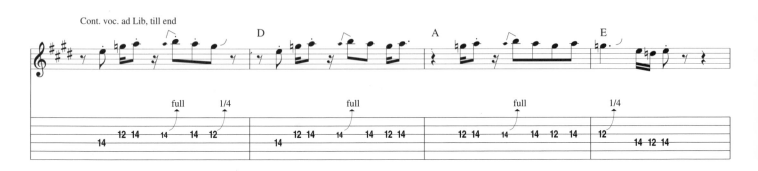
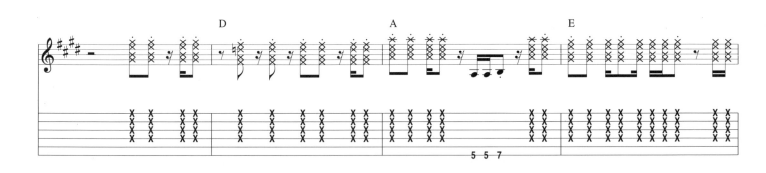
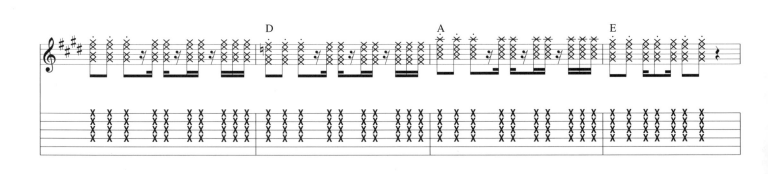
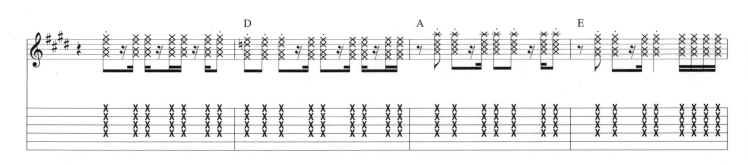

Salt of the Earth

Words and Music by Mick Jagger and Keith Richards

Performed by THE ROLLING STONES

MICK JAGGER: "And now, there's nothing left for us to say really, but to sing you one last goodnightly song and to wish you all.. goodnight."

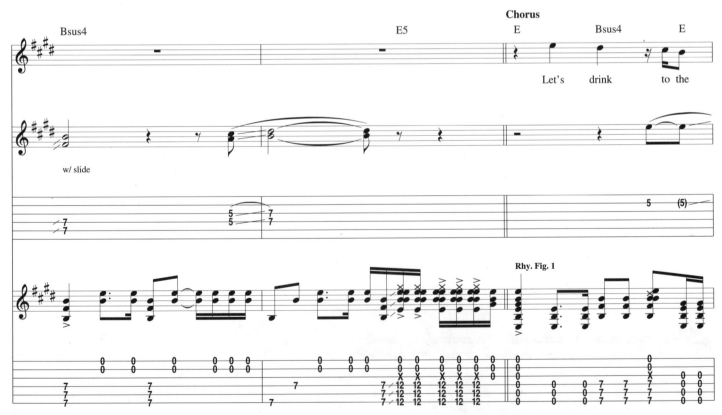

© 1968 ABKCO Music, Inc. (Copyright Renewed)
1700 Broadway, New York, NY 10019
International Copyright Secured   All Rights Reserved

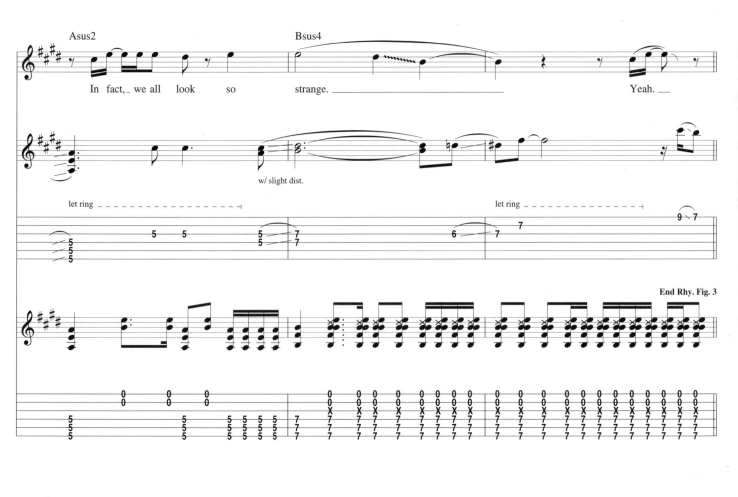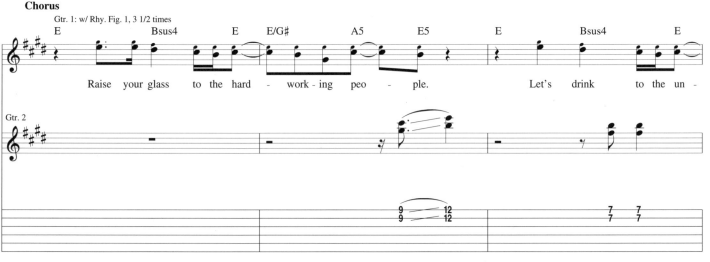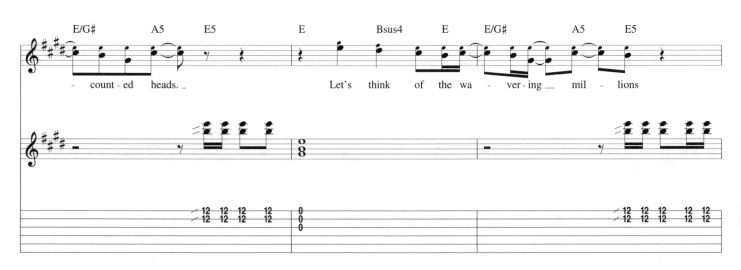

Guitar Notation Legend

Guitar Music can be notated three different ways: on a *musical staff*, in *tablature*, and in *rhythm slashes*.

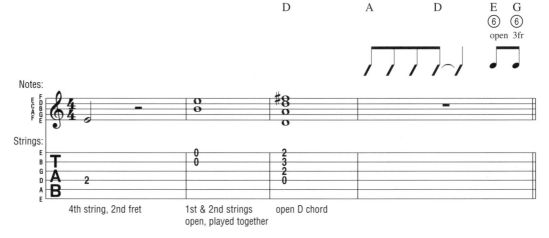

RHYTHM SLASHES are written above the staff. Strum chords in the rhythm indicated. Use the chord diagrams found at the top of the first page of the transcription for the appropriate chord voicings. Round noteheads indicate single notes.

THE MUSICAL STAFF shows pitches and rhythms and is divided by bar lines into measures. Pitches are named after the first seven letters of the alphabet.

TABLATURE graphically represents the guitar fingerboard. Each horizontal line represents a a string, and each number represents a fret.

Definitions for Special Guitar Notation

HALF-STEP BEND: Strike the note and bend up 1/2 step.

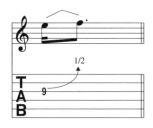

WHOLE-STEP BEND: Strike the note and bend up one step.

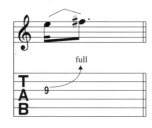

GRACE NOTE BEND: Strike the note and bend up as indicated. The first note does not take up any time.

SLIGHT (MICROTONE) BEND: Strike the note and bend up 1/4 step.

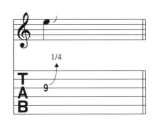

BEND AND RELEASE: Strike the note and bend up as indicated, then release back to the original note. Only the first note is struck.

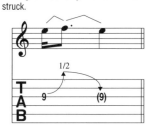

PRE-BEND: Bend the note as indicated, then strike it.

PRE-BEND AND RELEASE: Bend the note as indicated. Strike it and release the bend back to the original note.

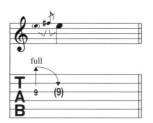

UNISON BEND: Strike the two notes simultaneously and bend the lower note up to the pitch of the higher.

VIBRATO: The string is vibrated by rapidly bending and releasing the note with the fretting hand.

WIDE VIBRATO: The pitch is varied to a greater degree by vibrating with the fretting hand.

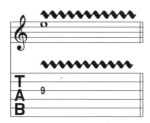

HAMMER-ON: Strike the first (lower) note with one finger, then sound the higher note (on the same string) with another finger by fretting it without picking.

PULL-OFF: Place both fingers on the notes to be sounded. Strike the first note and without picking, pull the finger off to sound the second (lower) note.

LEGATO SLIDE: Strike the first note and then slide the same fret-hand finger up or down to the second note. The second note is not struck.

SHIFT SLIDE: Same as legato slide, except the second note is struck.

TRILL: Very rapidly alternate between the notes indicated by continuously hammering on and pulling off.

TAPPING: Hammer ("tap") the fret indicated with the pick-hand index or middle finger and pull off to the note fretted by the fret hand.

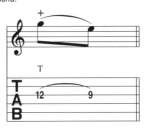

NATURAL HARMONIC: Strike the note while the fret-hand lightly touches the string directly over the fret indicated.

PINCH HARMONIC: The note is fretted normally and a harmonic is produced by adding the edge of the thumb or the tip of the index finger of the pick hand to the normal pick attack.

HARP HARMONIC: The note is fretted normally and a harmonic is produced by gently resting the pick hand's index finger directly above the indicated fret (in parentheses) while the pick hand's thumb or pick assists by plucking the appropriate string.

PICK SCRAPE: The edge of the pick is rubbed down (or up) the string, producing a scratchy sound.

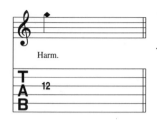 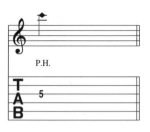  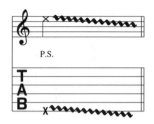

MUFFLED STRINGS: A percussive sound is produced by laying the fret hand across the string(s) without depressing, and striking them with the pick hand.

PALM MUTING: The note is partially muted by the pick hand lightly touching the string(s) just before the bridge.

RAKE: Drag the pick across the strings indicated with a single motion.

TREMOLO PICKING: The note is picked as rapidly and continuously as possible.

ARPEGGIATE: Play the notes of the chord indicated by quickly rolling them from bottom to top.

VIBRATO BAR DIVE AND RETURN: The pitch of the note or chord is dropped a specified number of steps (in rhythm) then returned to the original pitch.

VIBRATO BAR SCOOP: Depress the bar just before striking the note, then quickly release the bar.

VIBRATO BAR DIP: Strike the note and then immediately drop a specified number of steps, then release back to the original pitch.

 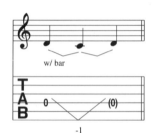  

Additional Musical Definitions

(accent)	• Accentuate note (play it louder)	
(accent)	• Accentuate note with great intensity	
(staccato)	• Play the note short	
⊓	• Downstroke	
∨	• Upstroke	
D.S. al Coda	• Go back to the sign (𝄋), then play until the measure marked "*To Coda*," then skip to the section labelled "*Coda*."	
D.S. al Fine	• Go back to the beginning of the song and play until the measure marked "*Fine*" (end).	

Rhy. Fig.	• Label used to recall a recurring accompaniment pattern (usually chordal).
Riff	• Label used to recall composed, melodic lines (usually single notes) which recur.
Fill	• Label used to identify a brief melodic figure which is to be inserted into the arrangement.
Rhy. Fill	• A chordal version of a Fill.
tacet	• Instrument is silent (drops out).
	• Repeat measures between signs.
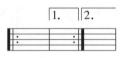	• When a repeated section has different endings, play the first ending only the first time and the second ending only the second time.

NOTE: Tablature numbers in parentheses mean:
1. The note is being sustained over a system (note in standard notation is tied), or
2. The note is sustained, but a new articulation (such as a hammer-on, pull-off, slide or vibrato begins, or
3. The note is a barely audible "ghost" note (note in standard notation is also in parentheses).